Laguna BEACH

GRAYSCALE COLORING BOOKS

VOLUME 1.

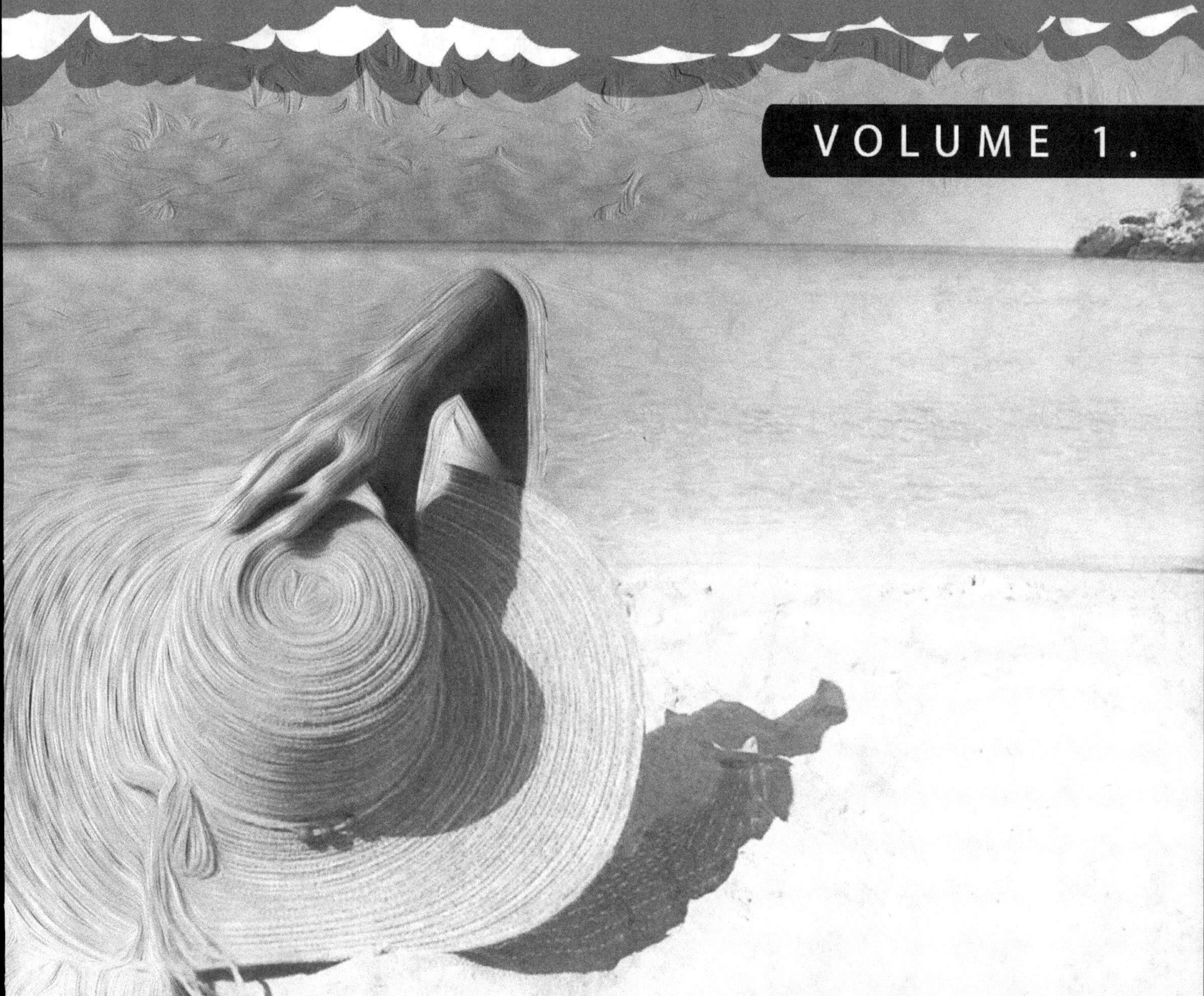

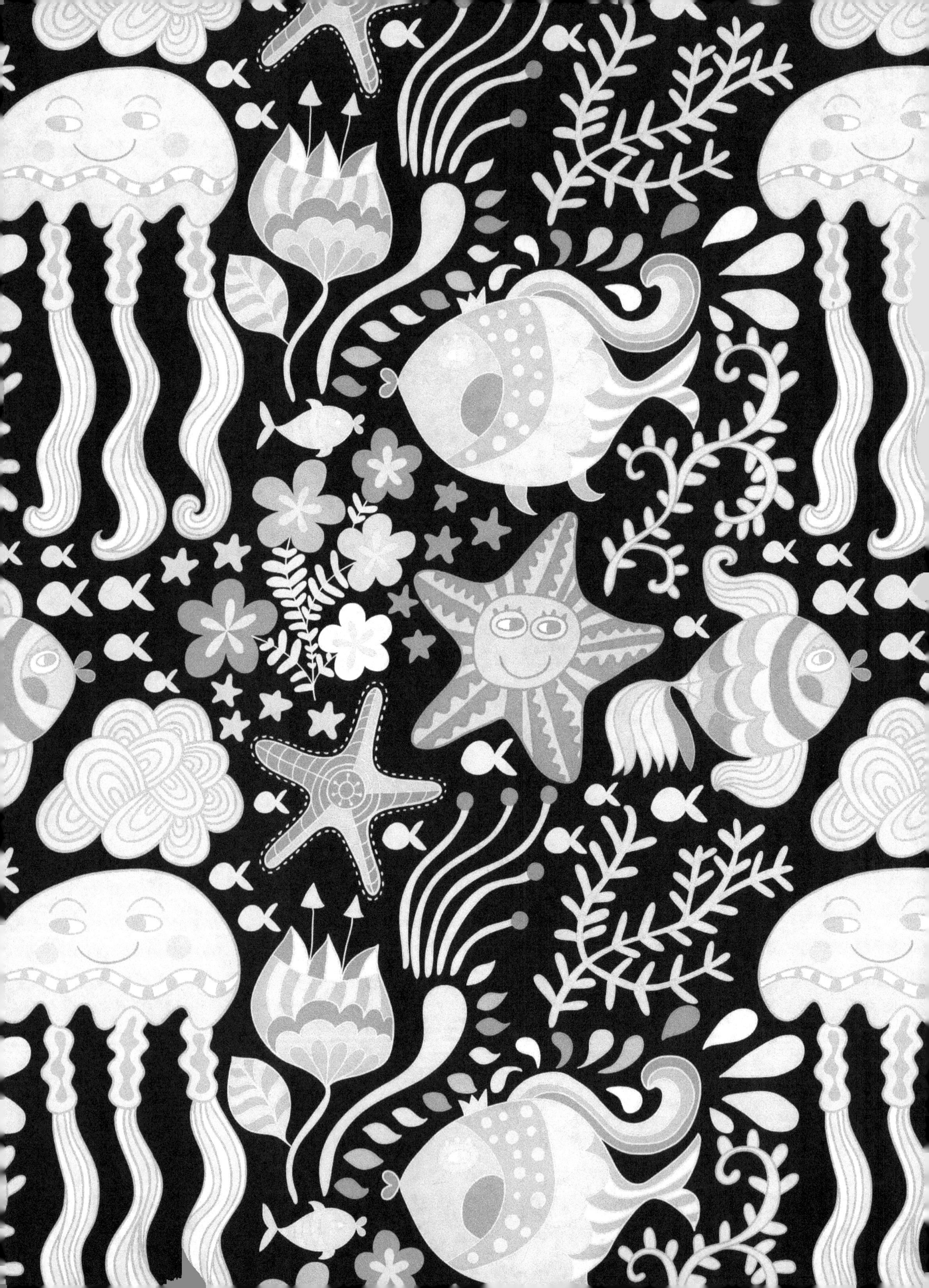

COLOR TEST PAGE

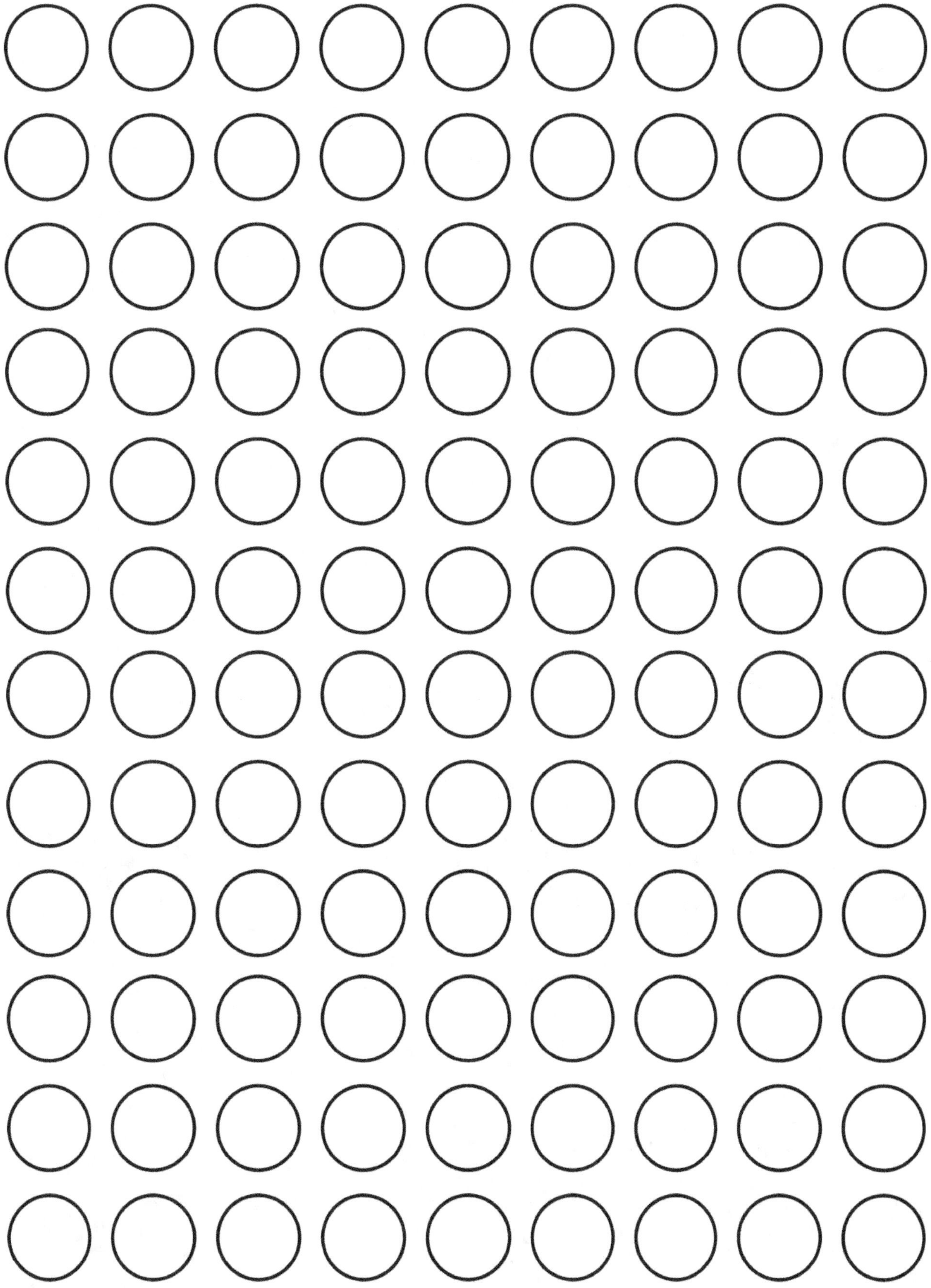

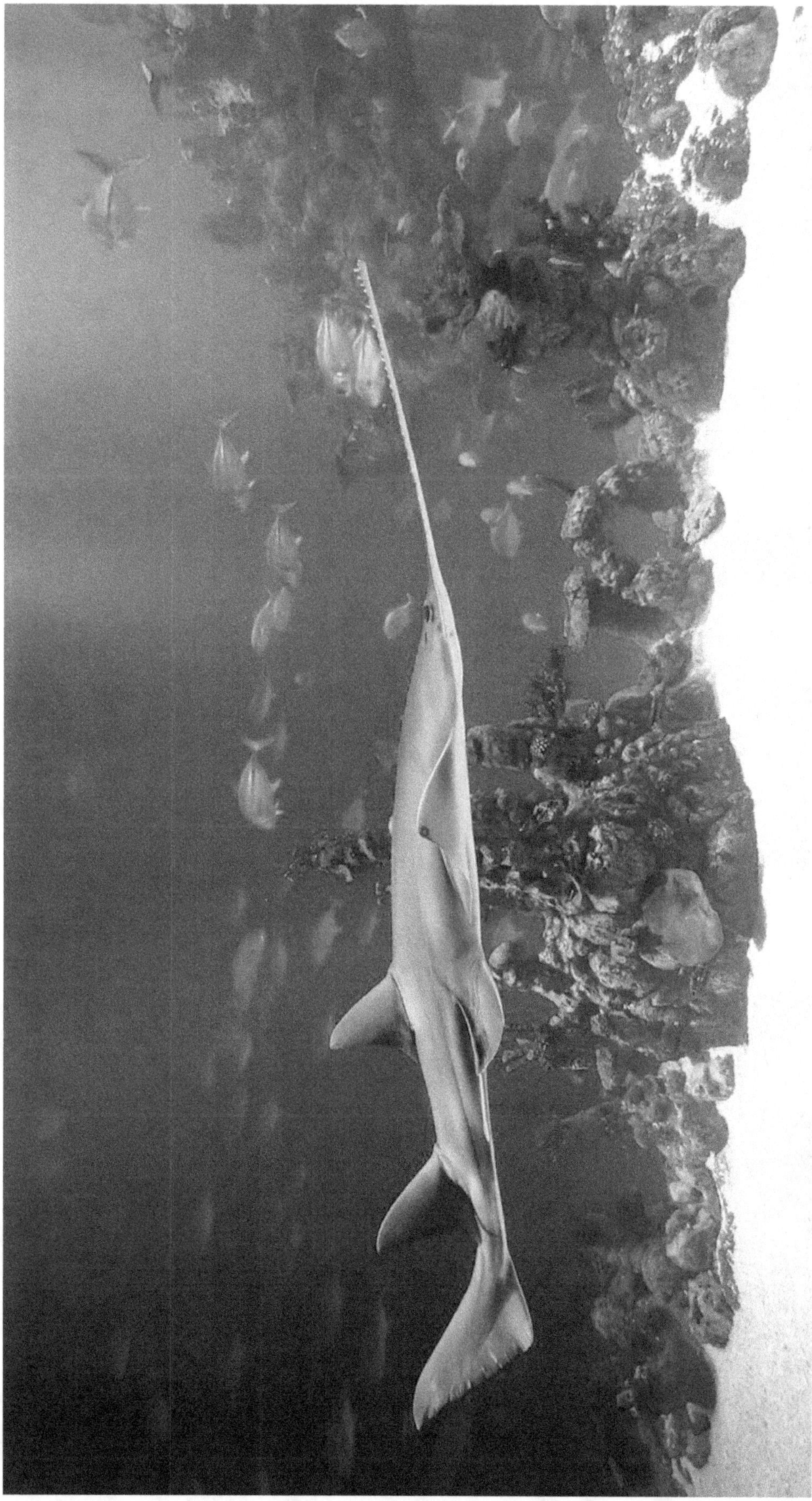

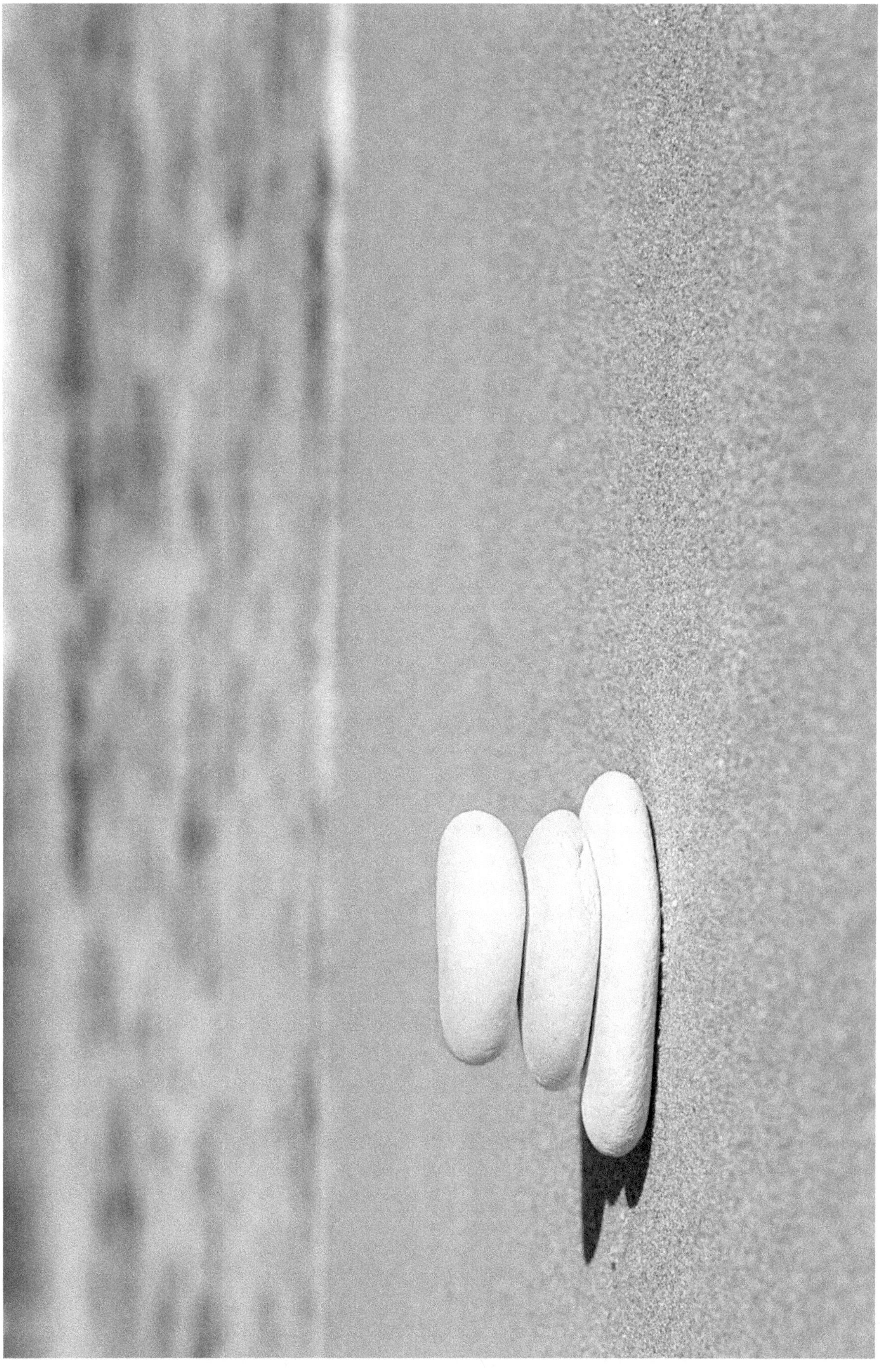

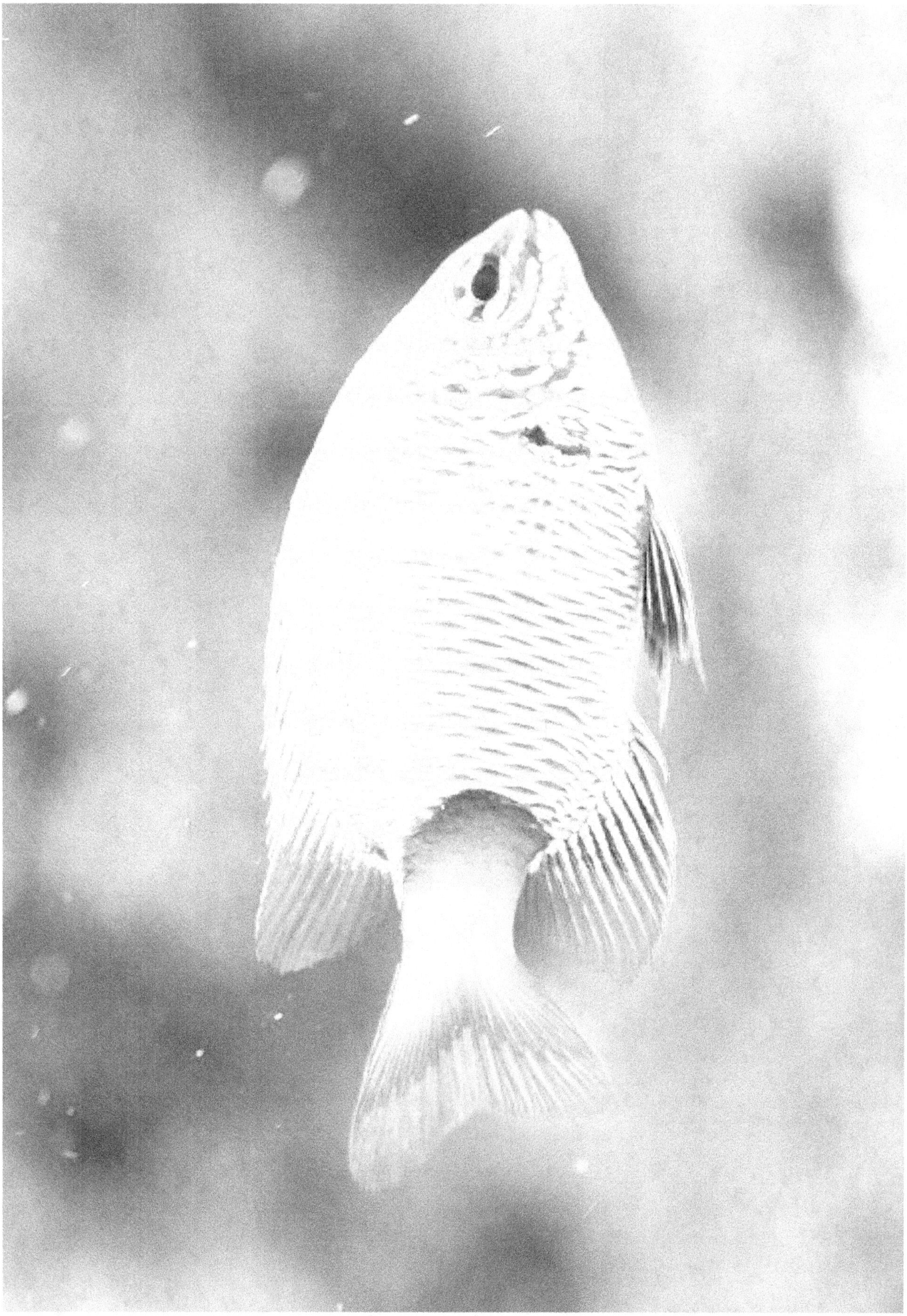

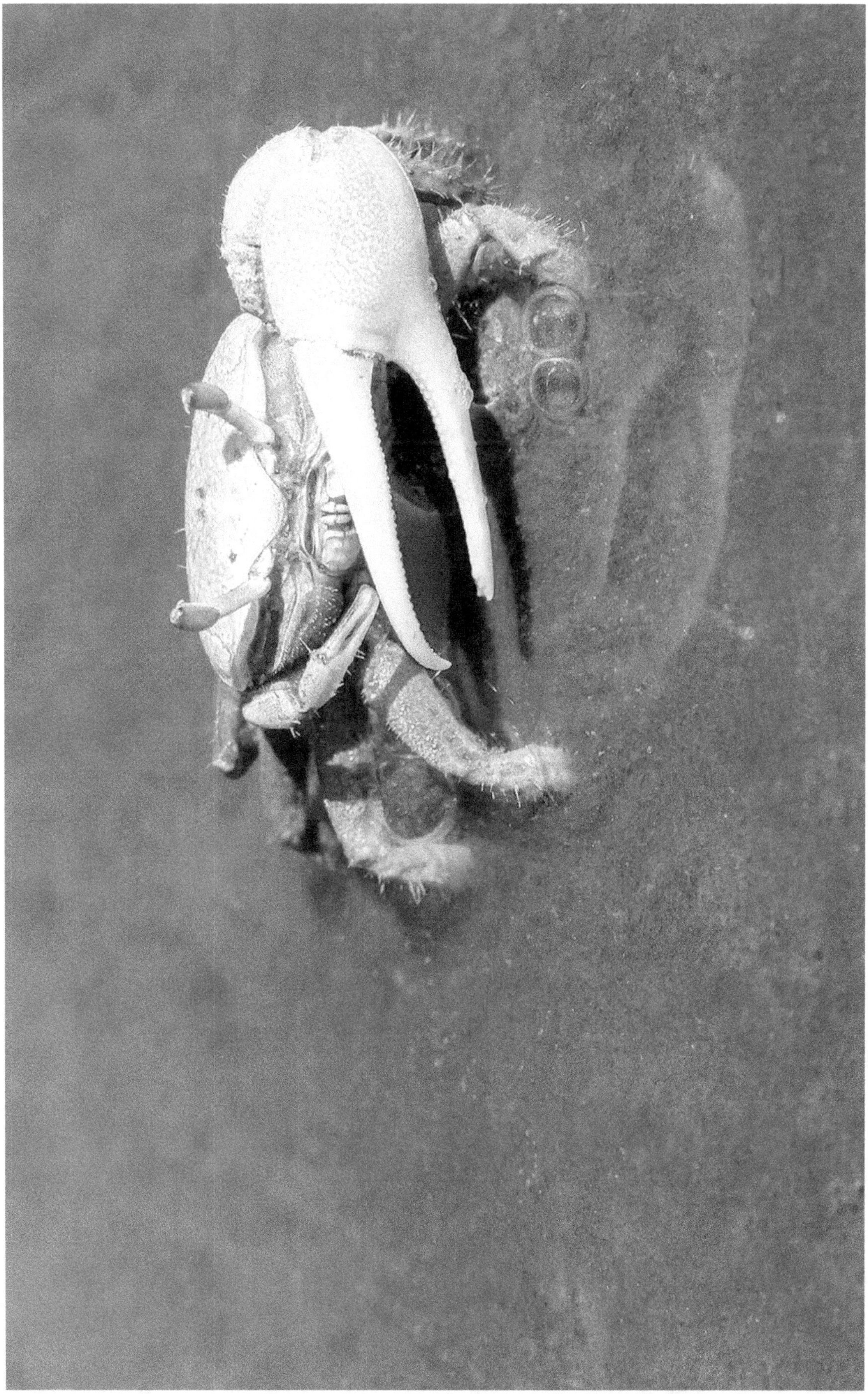

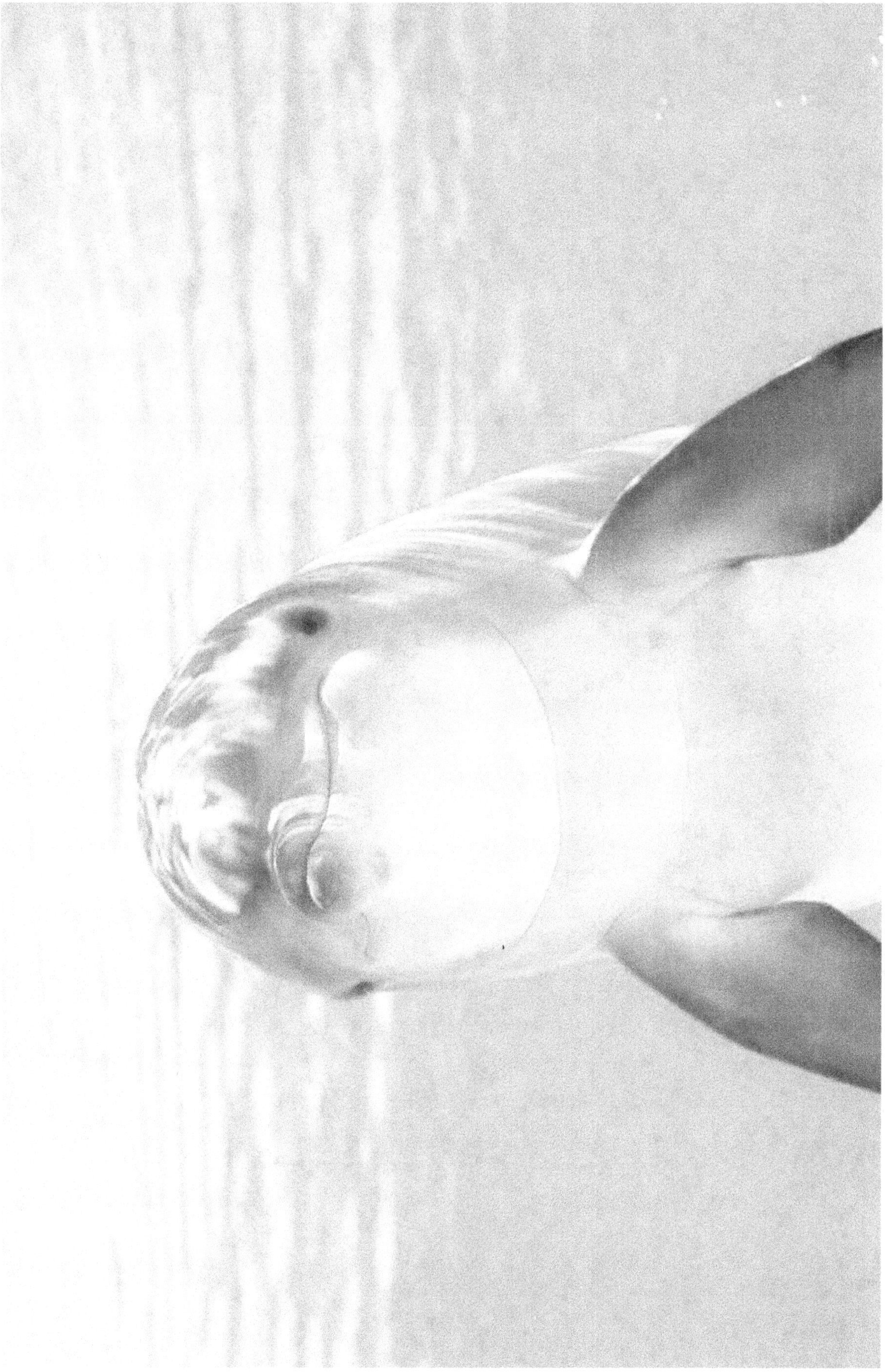

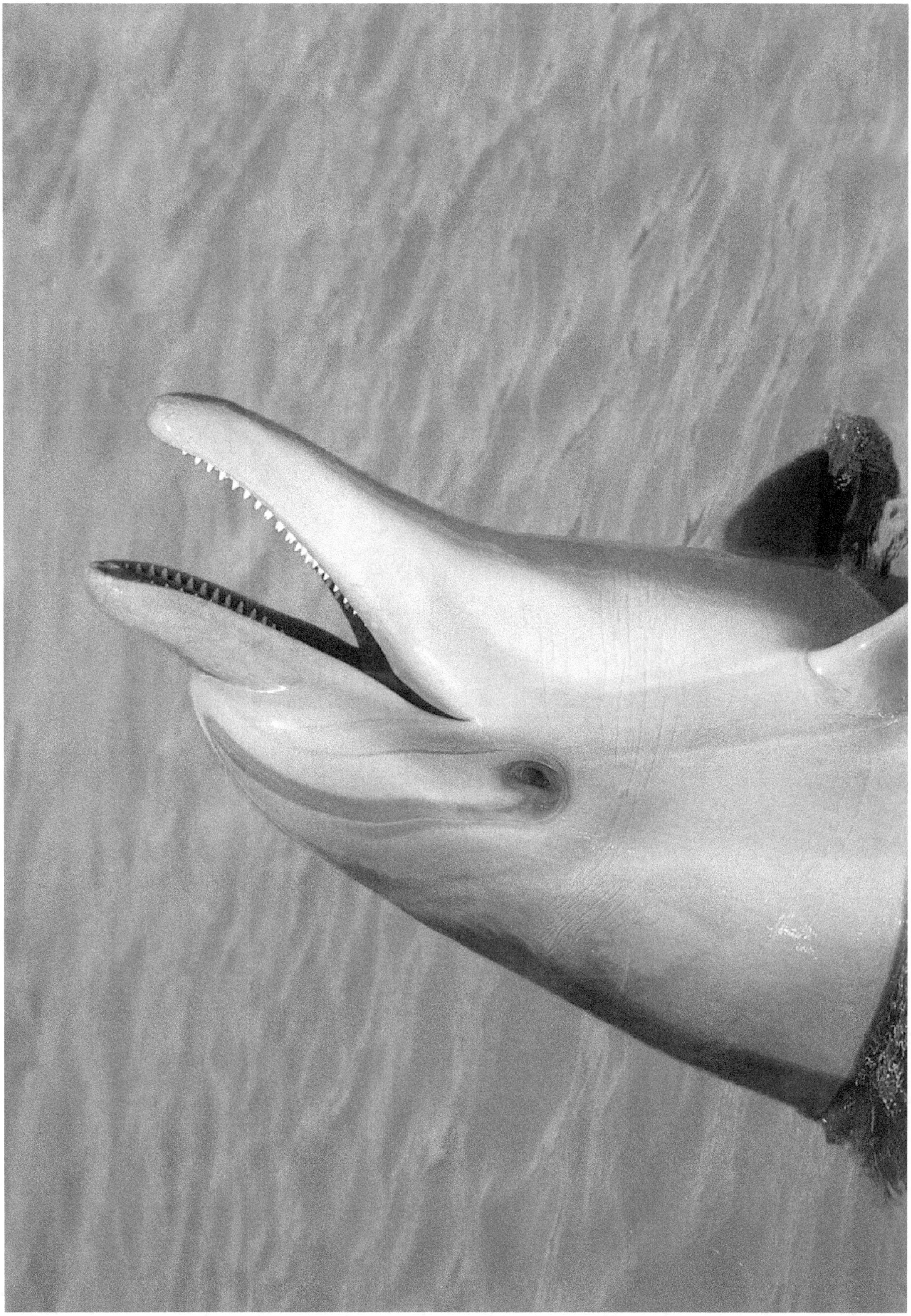

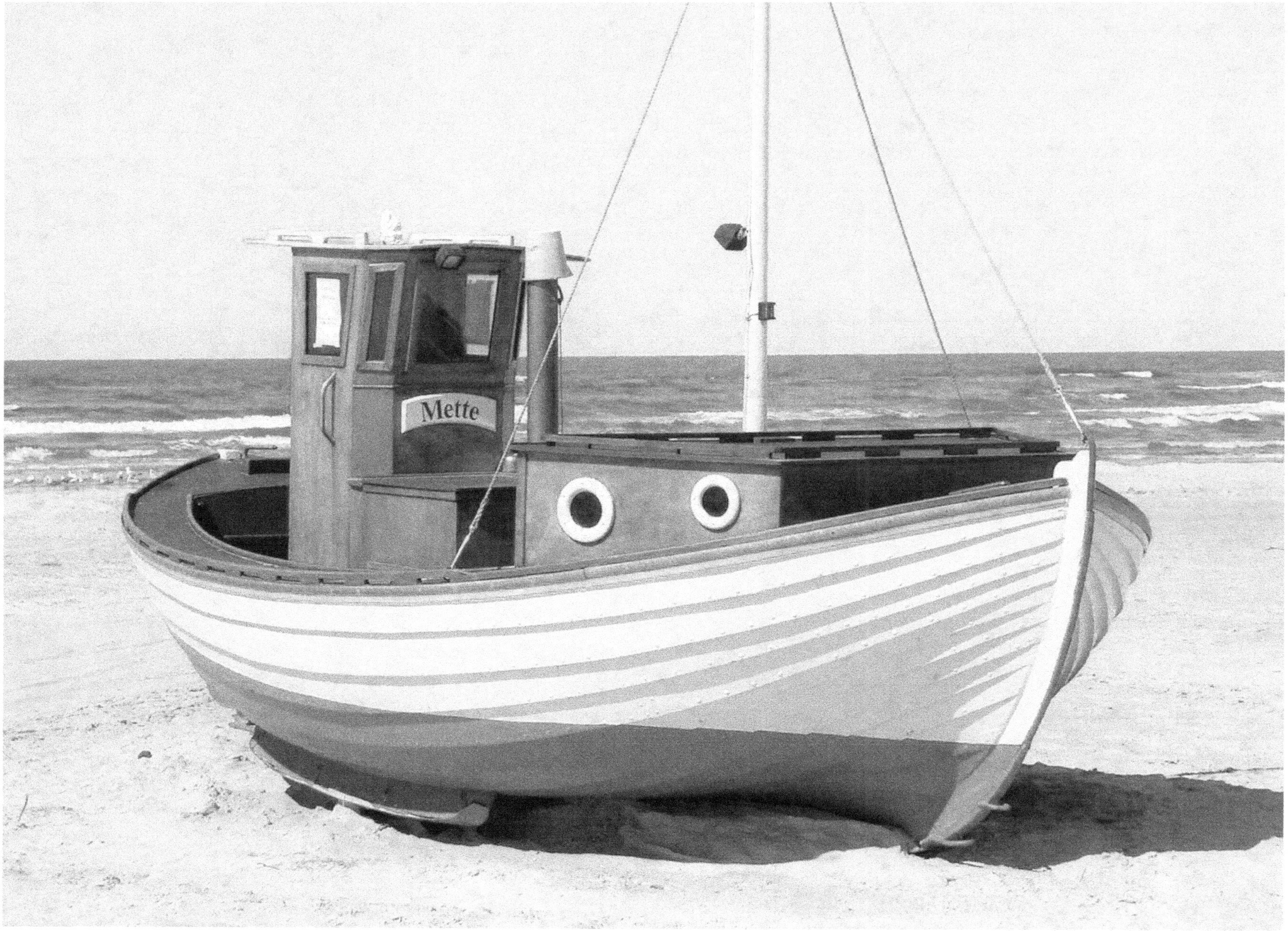
Mette

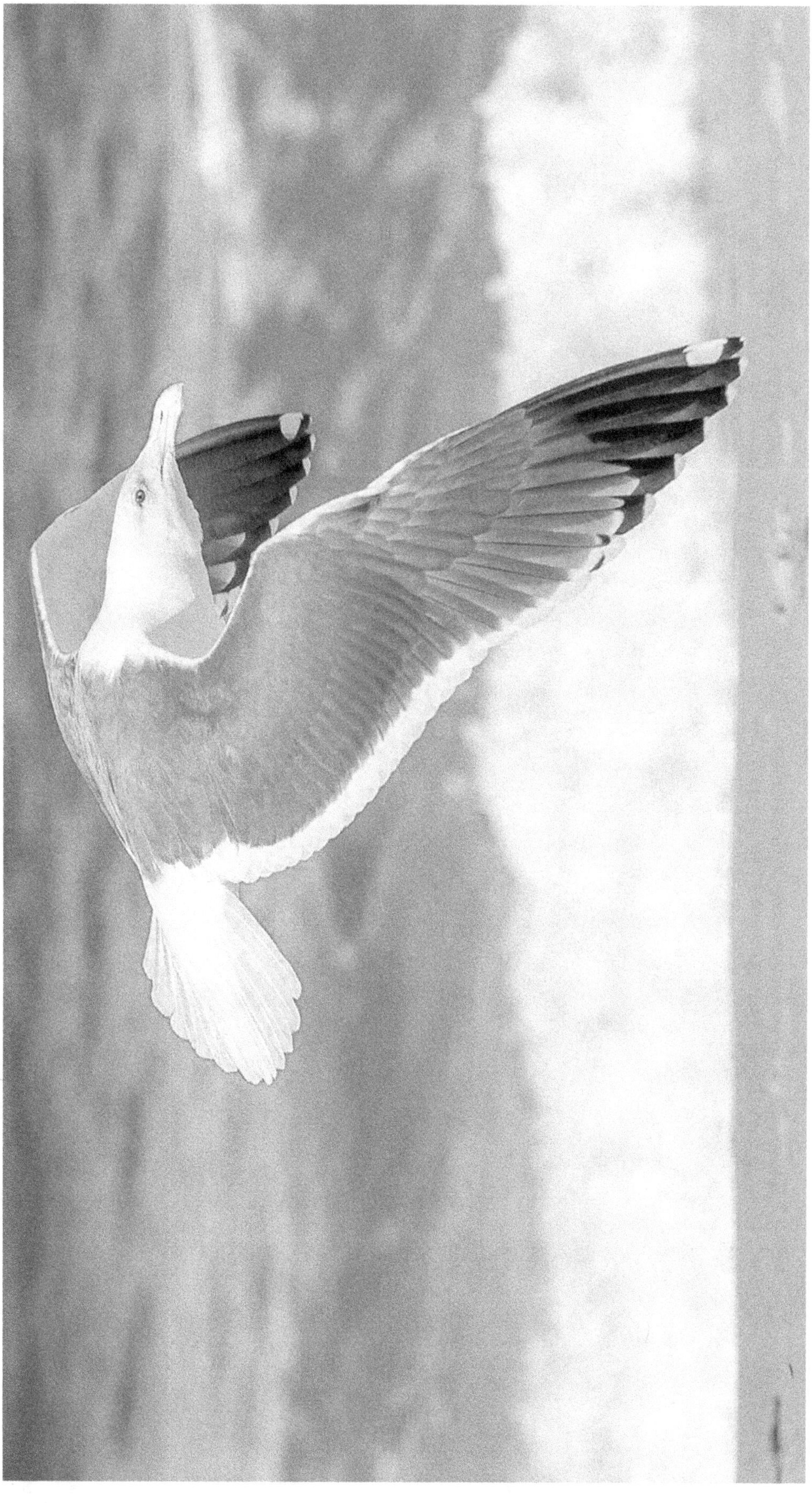

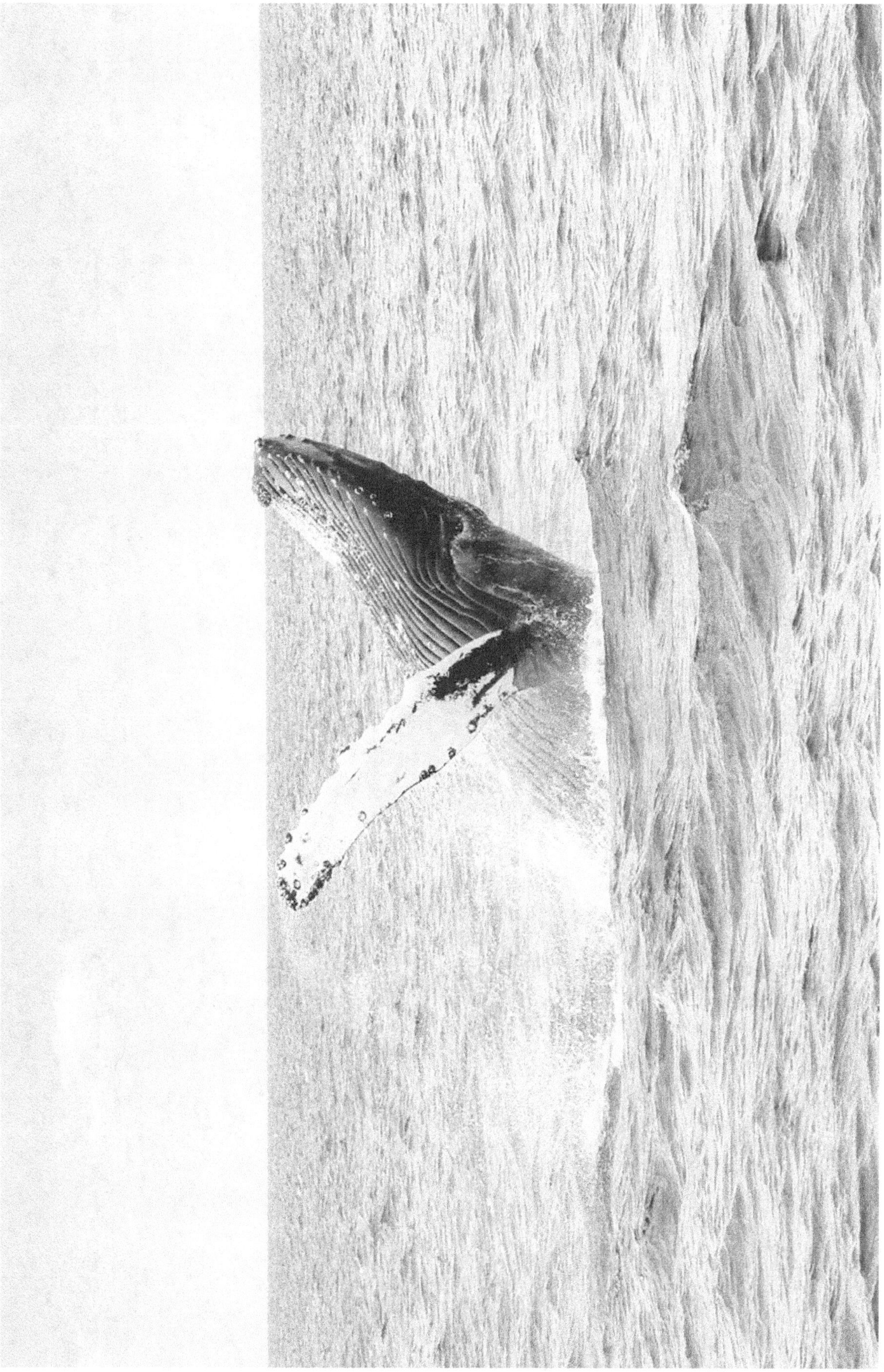

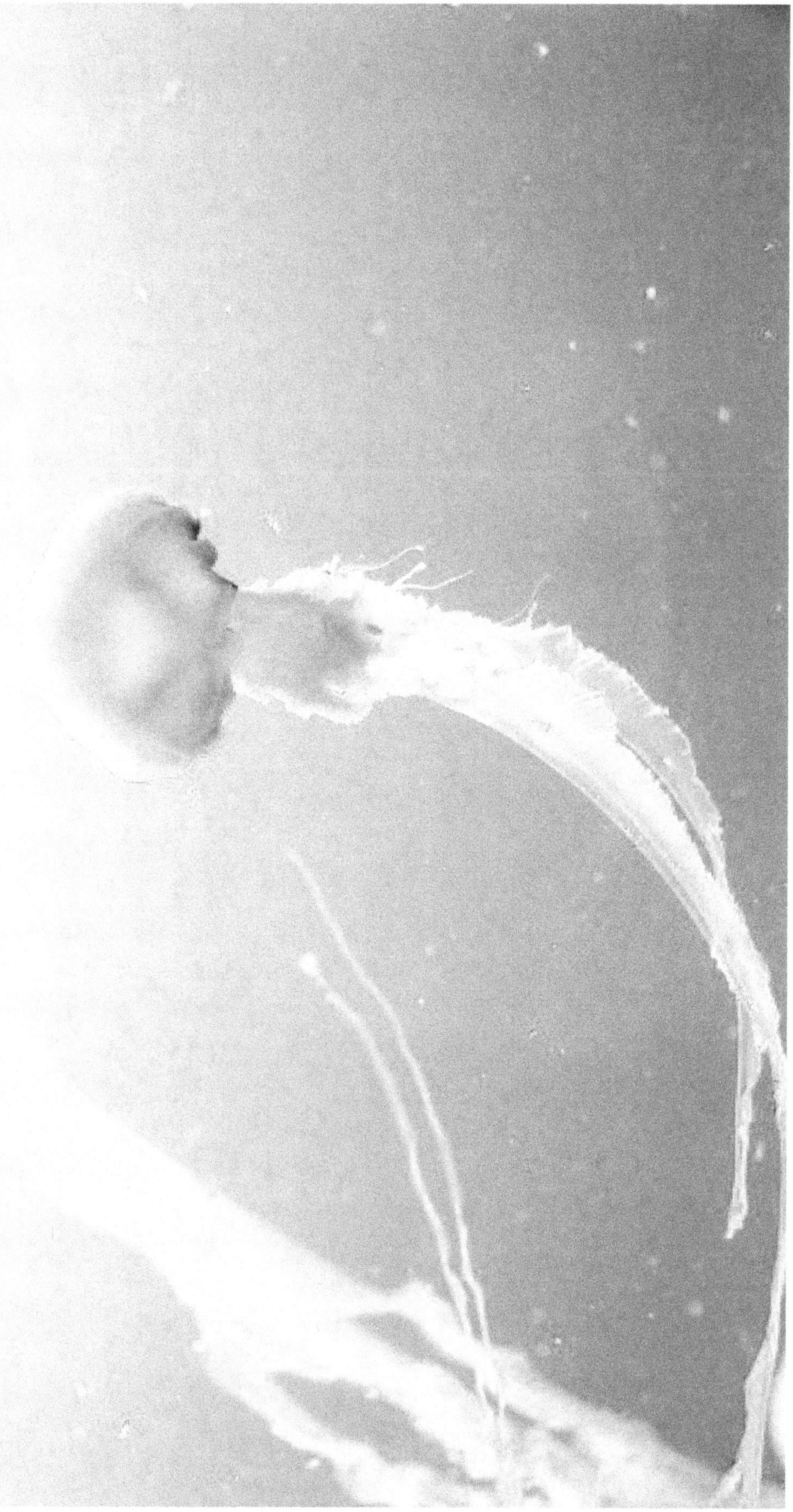

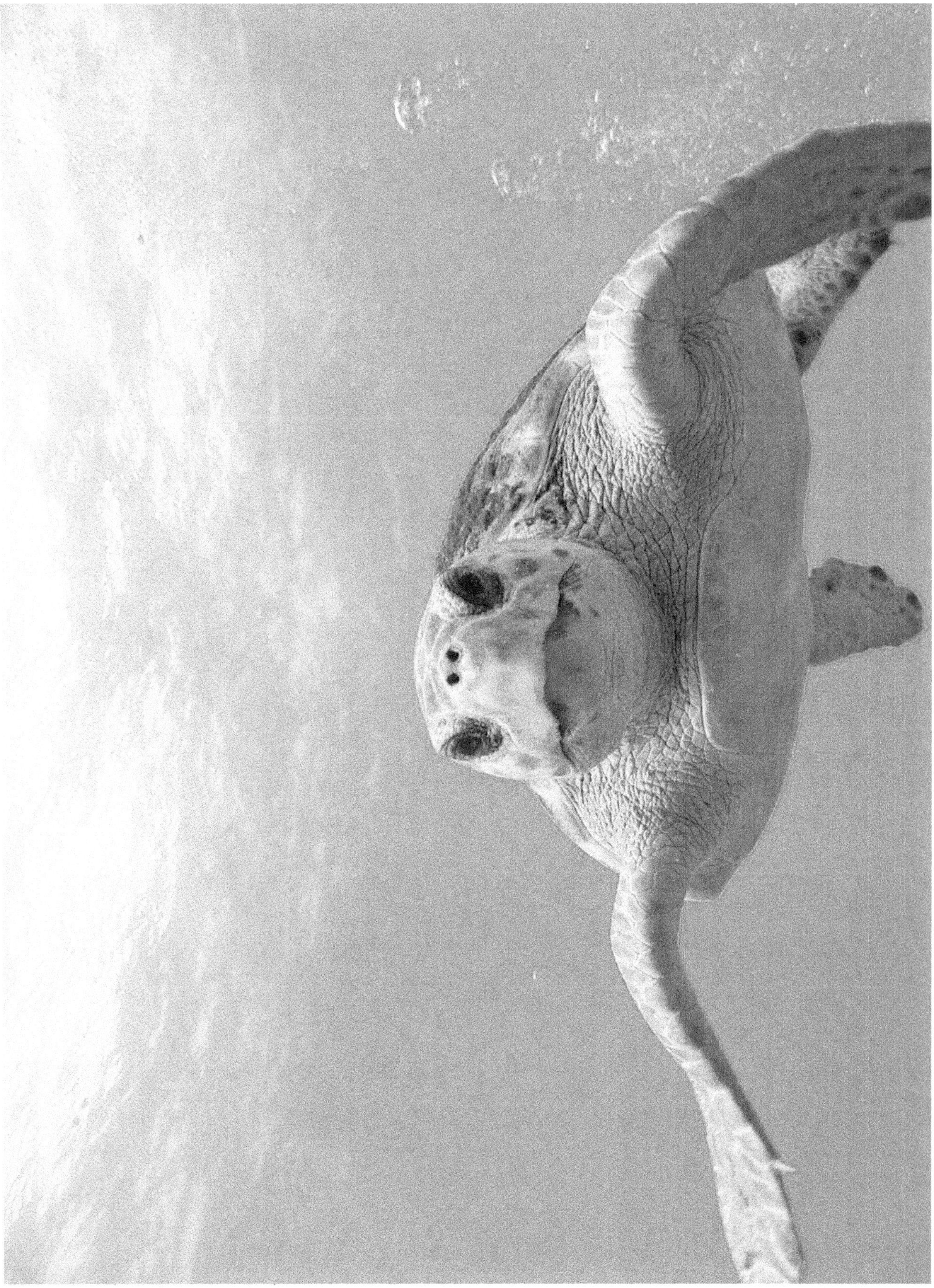

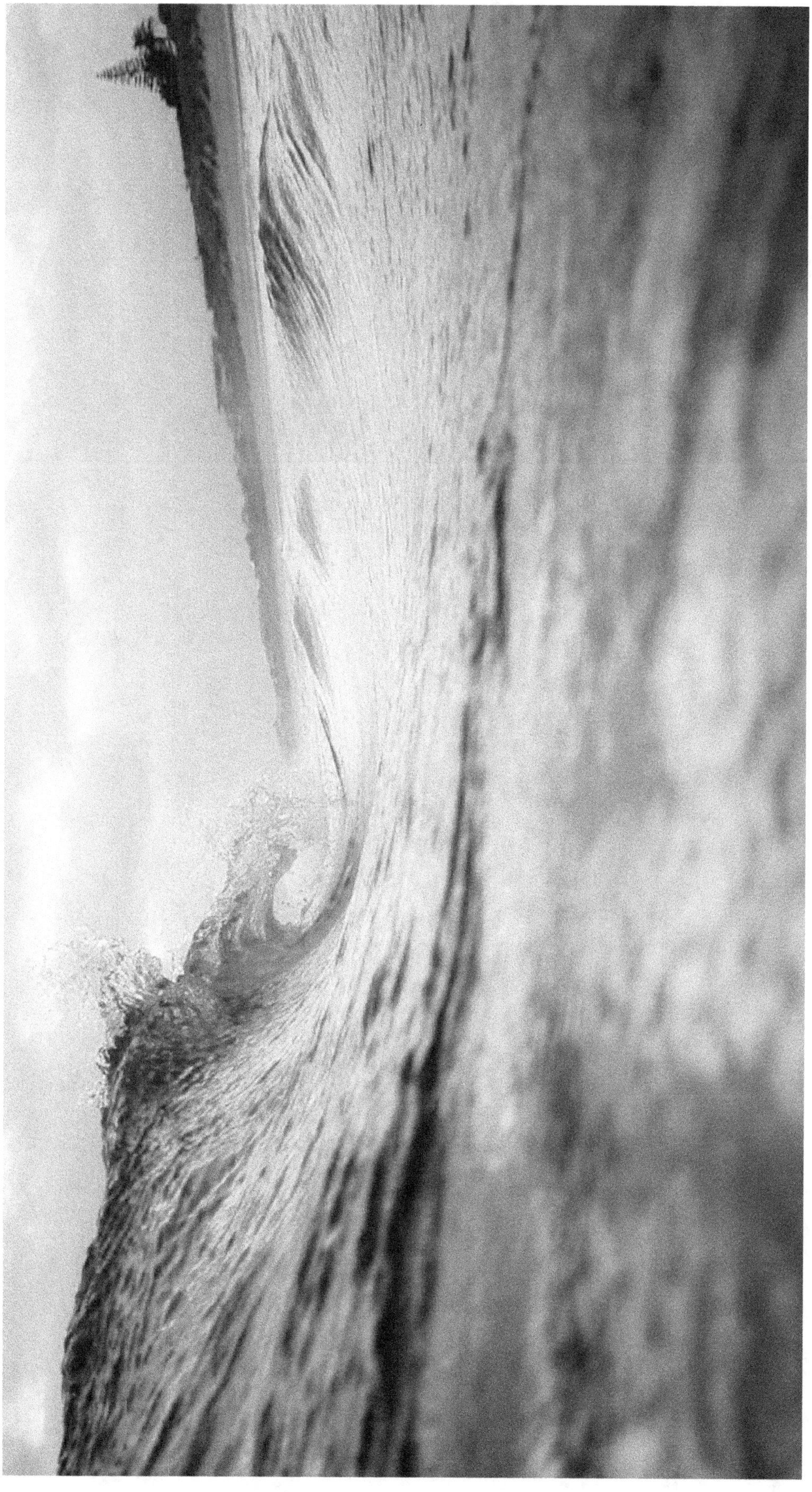

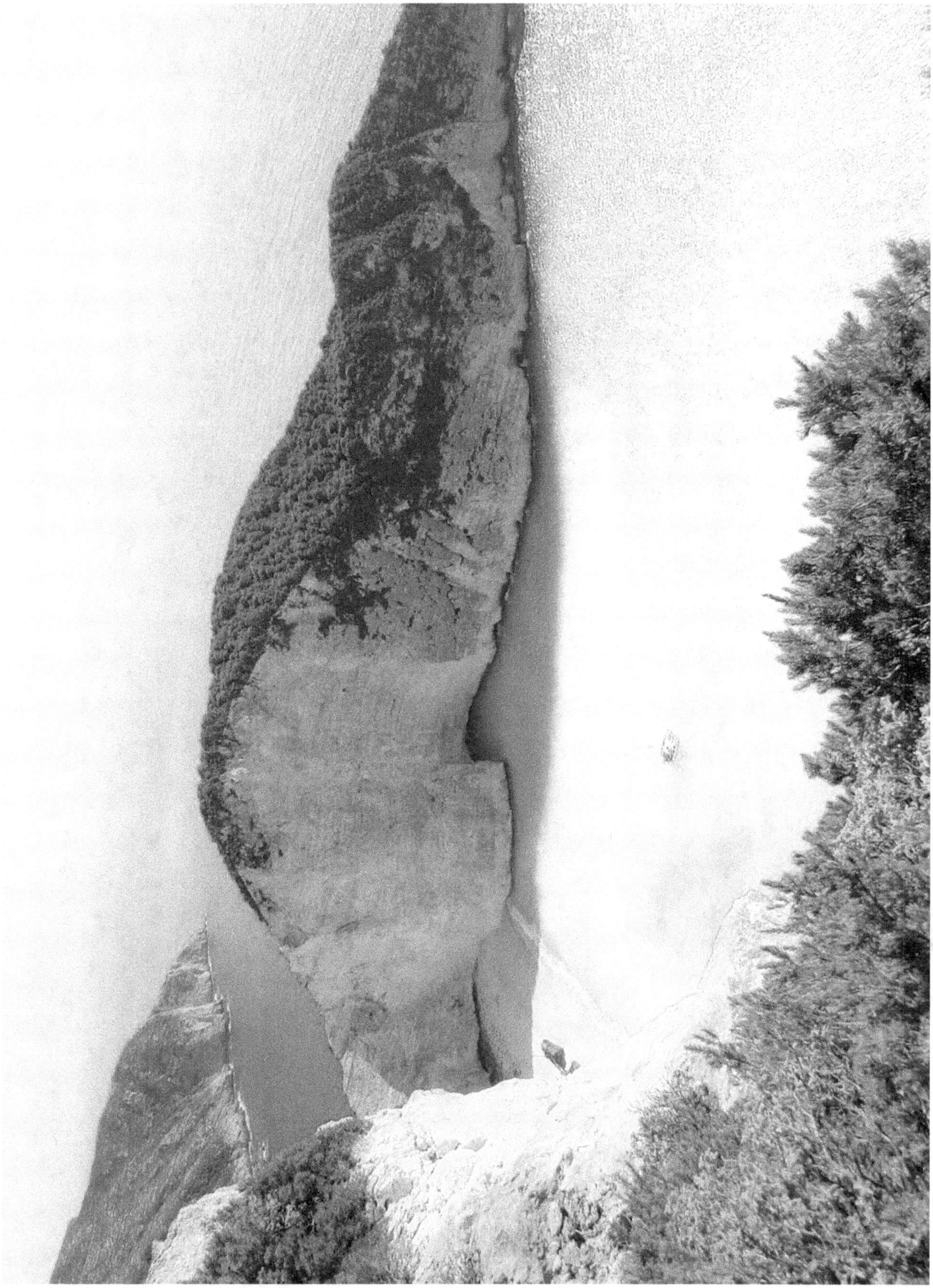

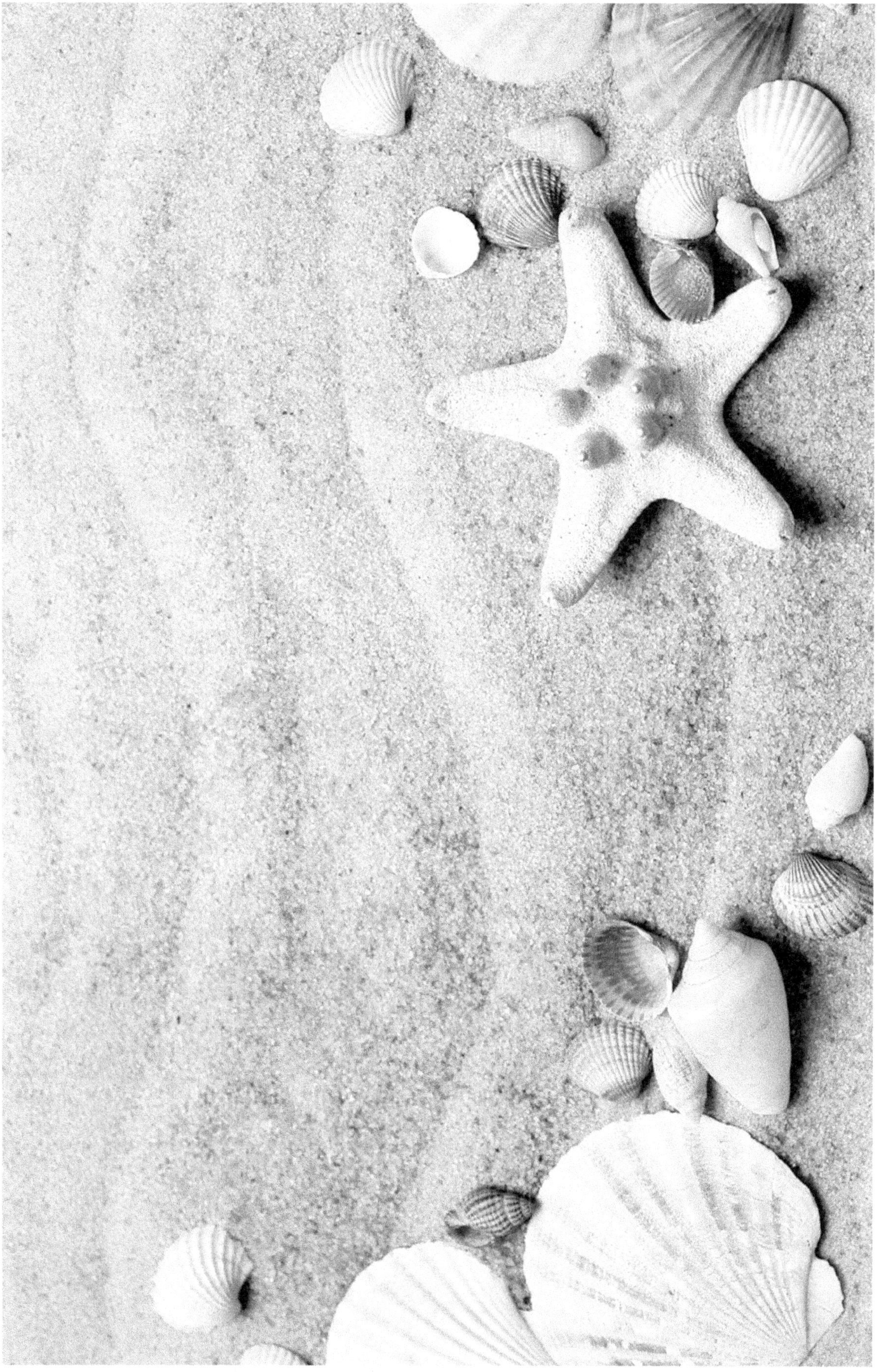

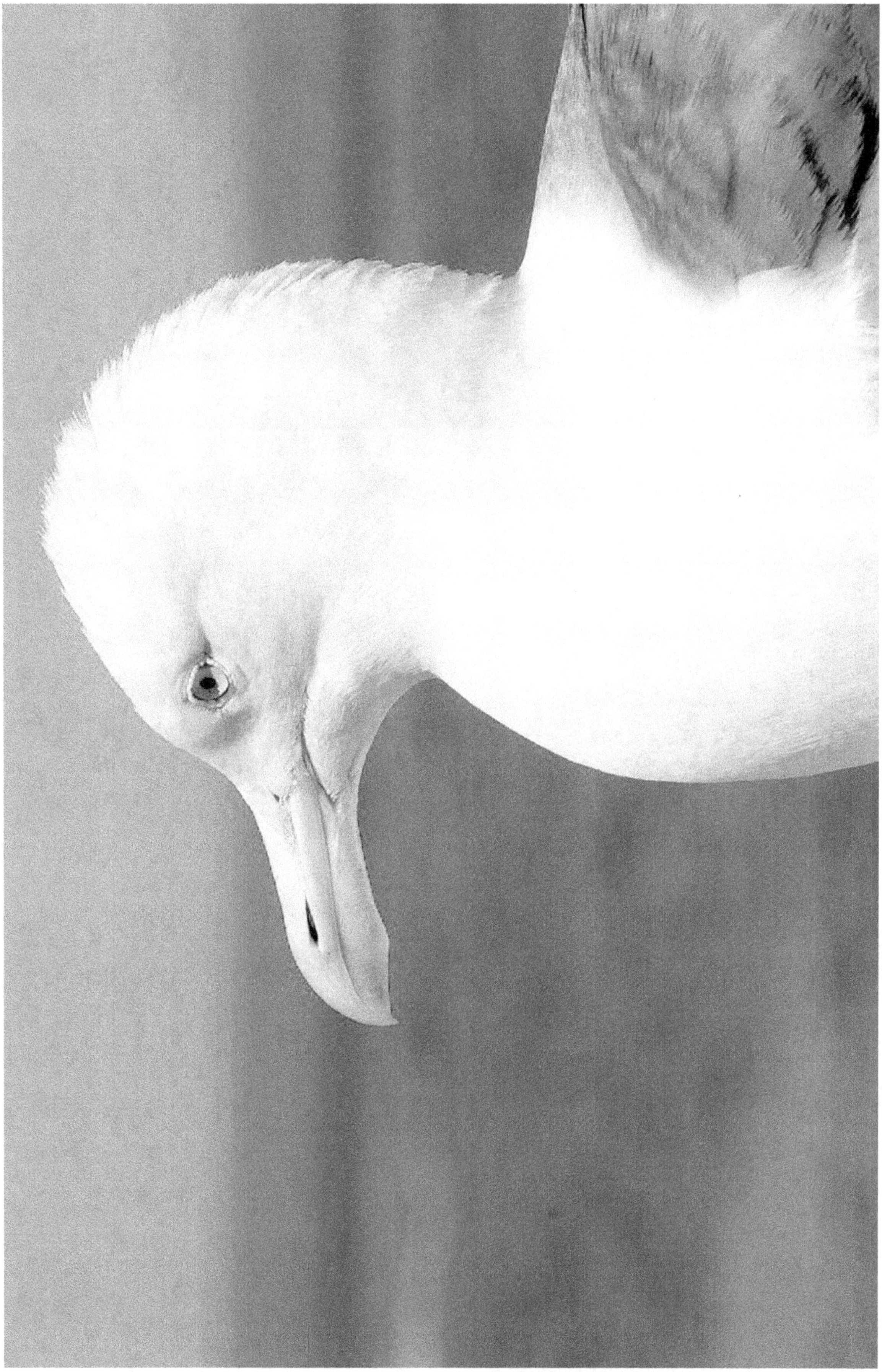

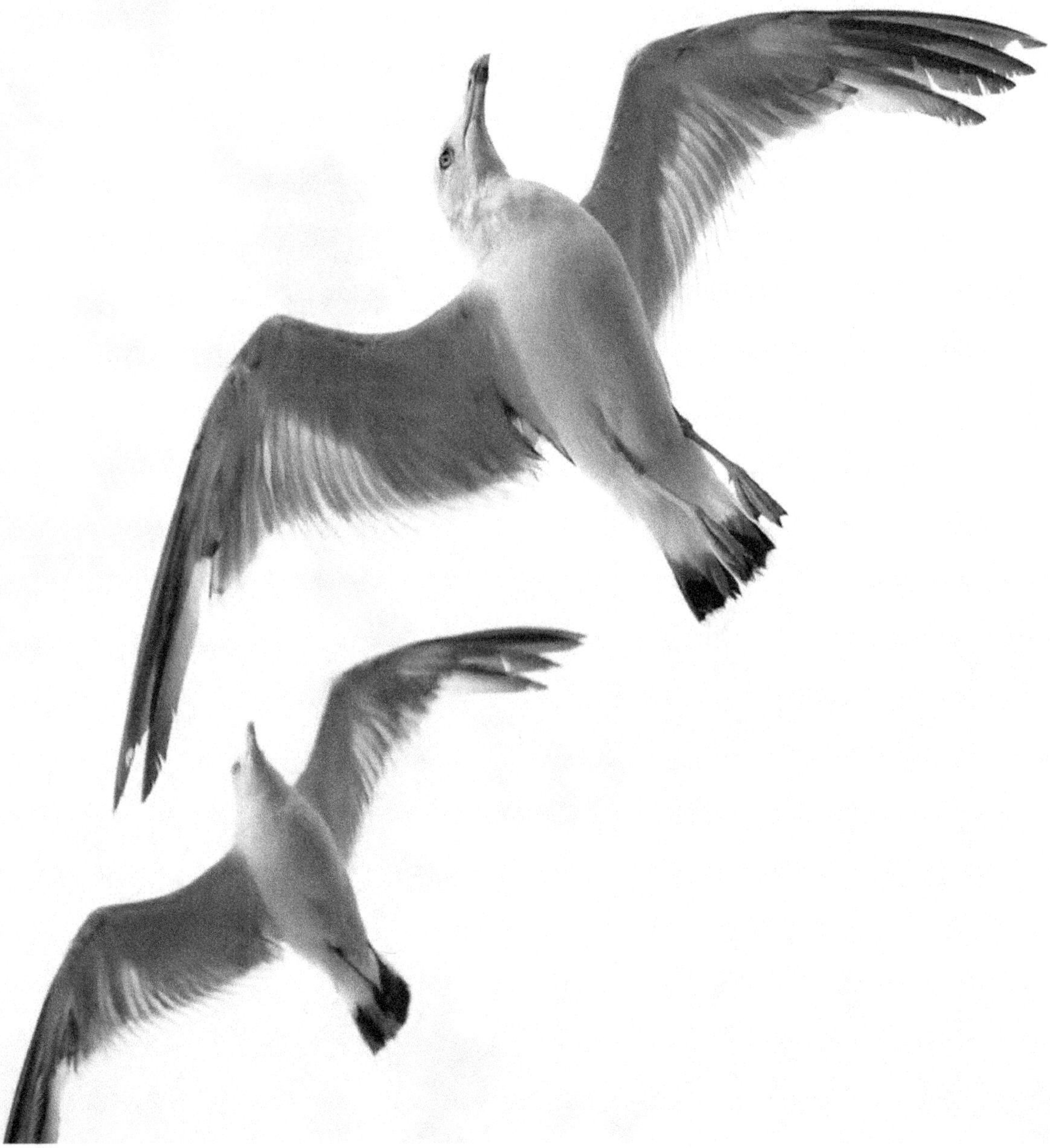

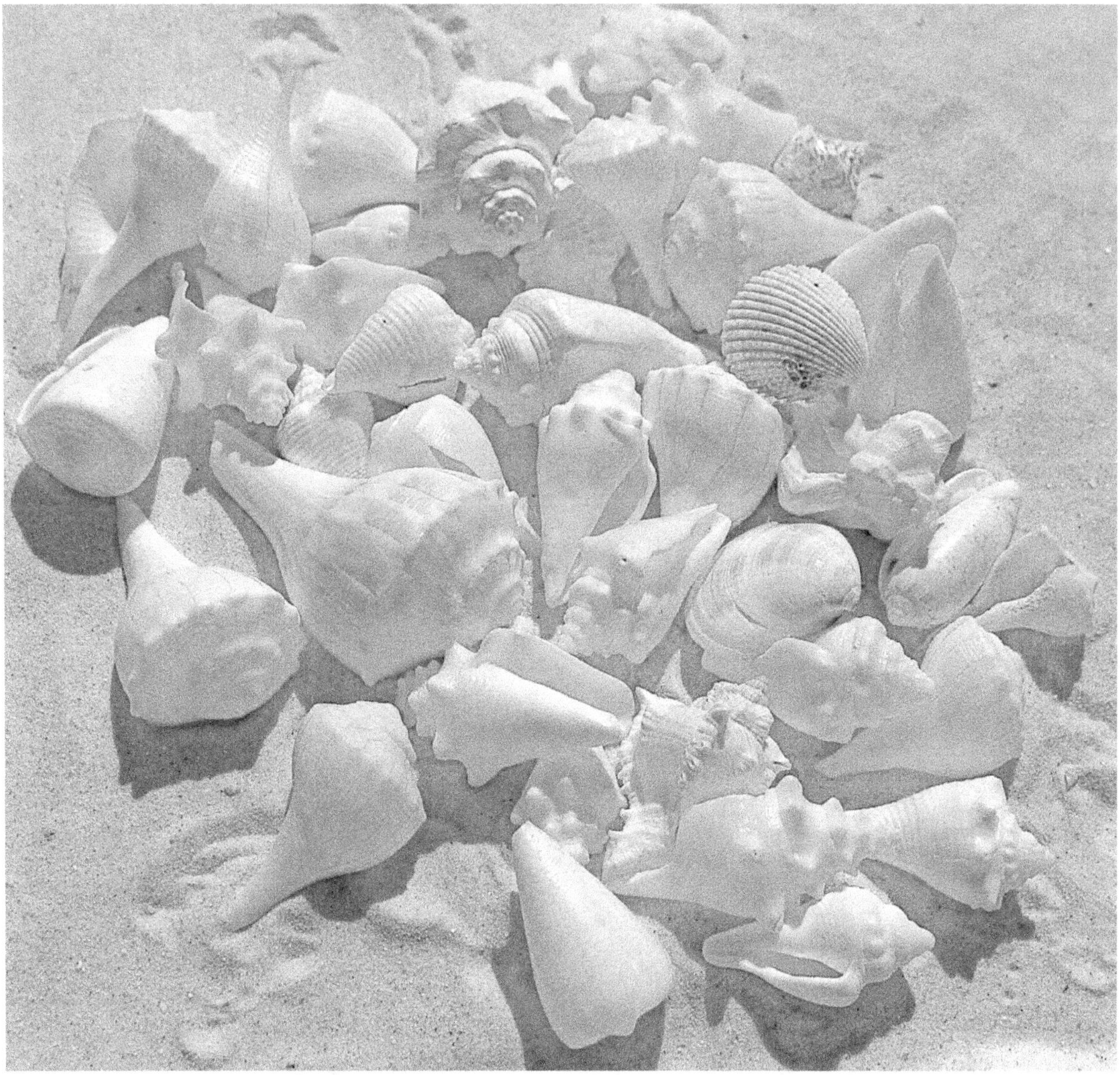

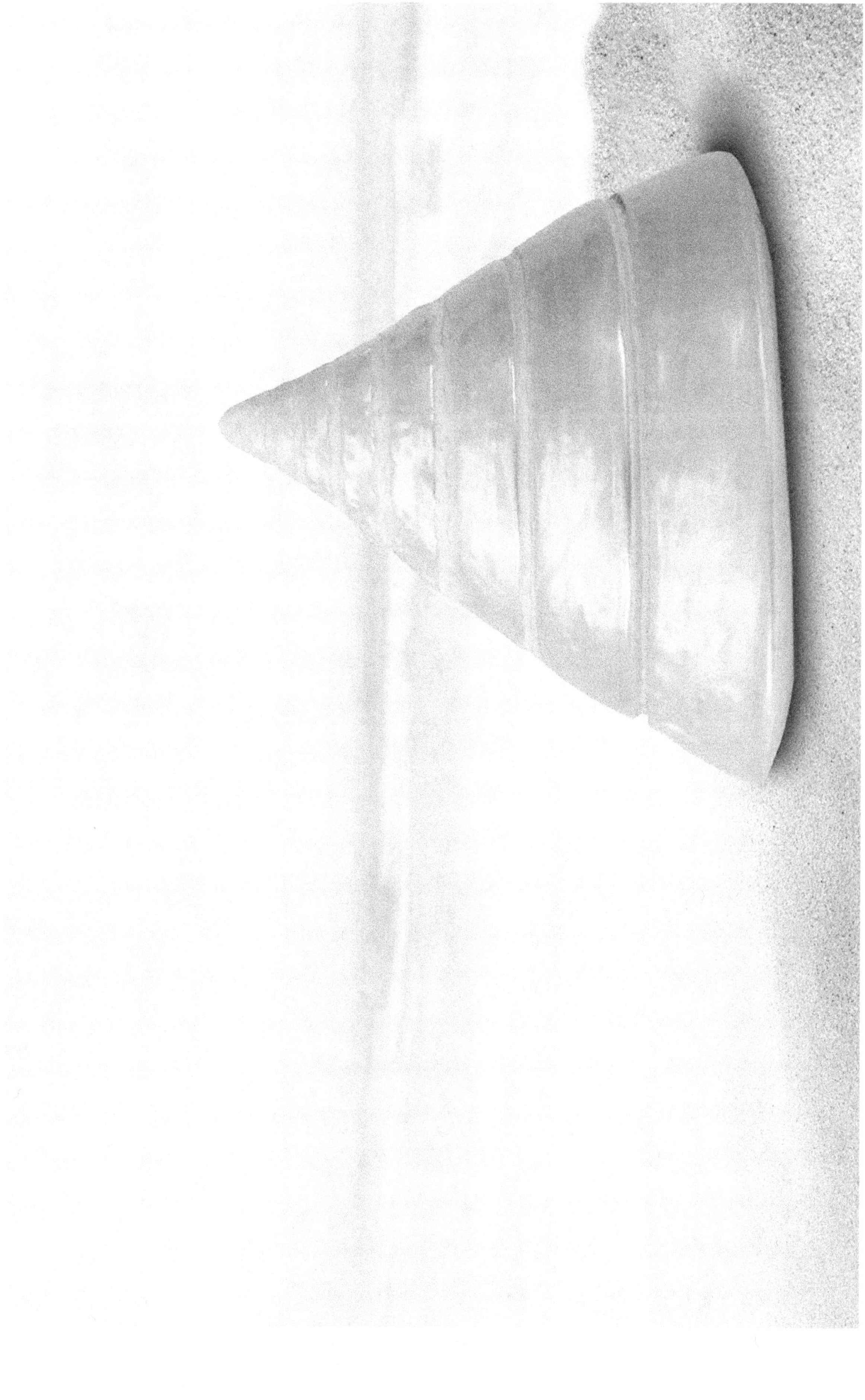

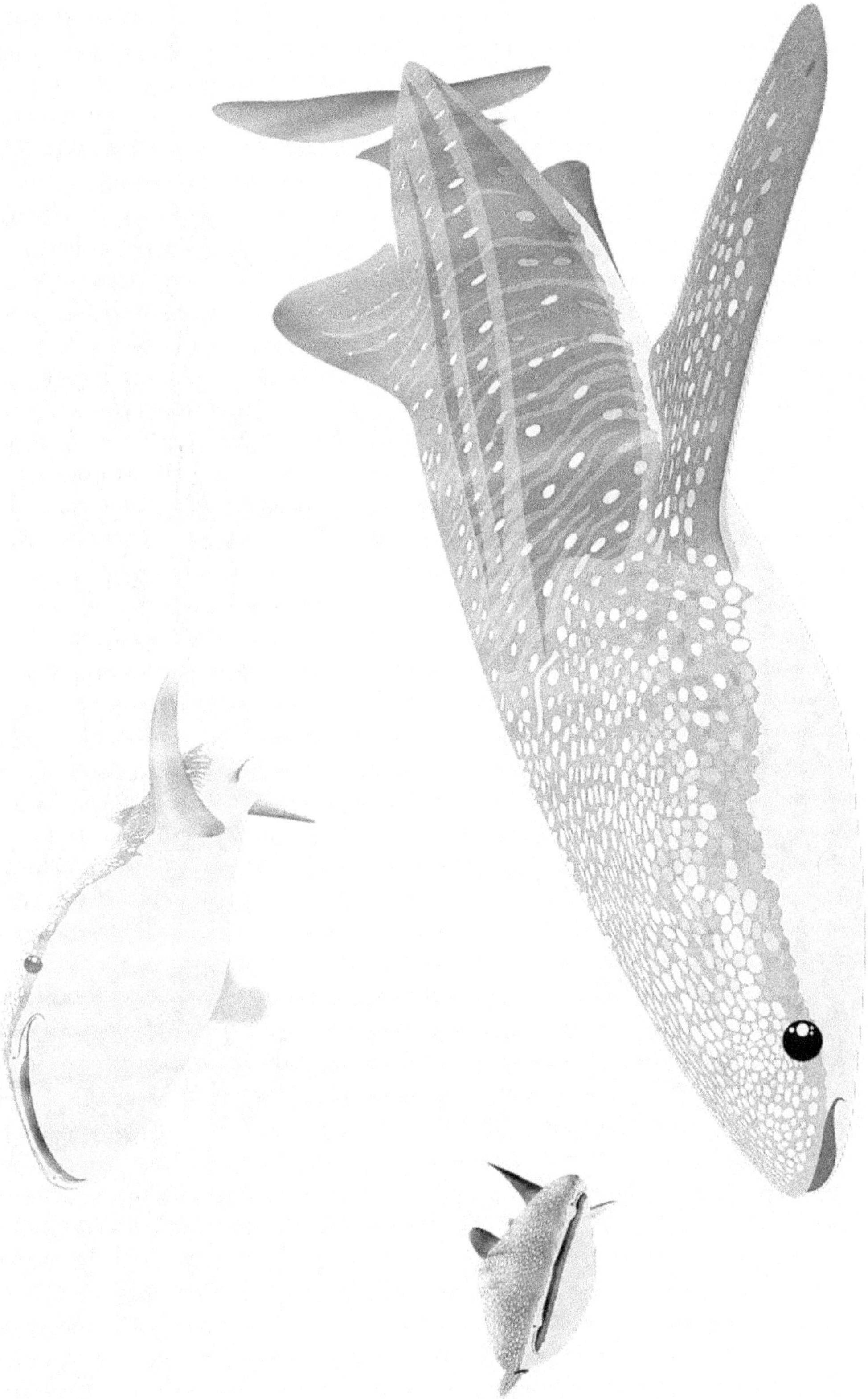

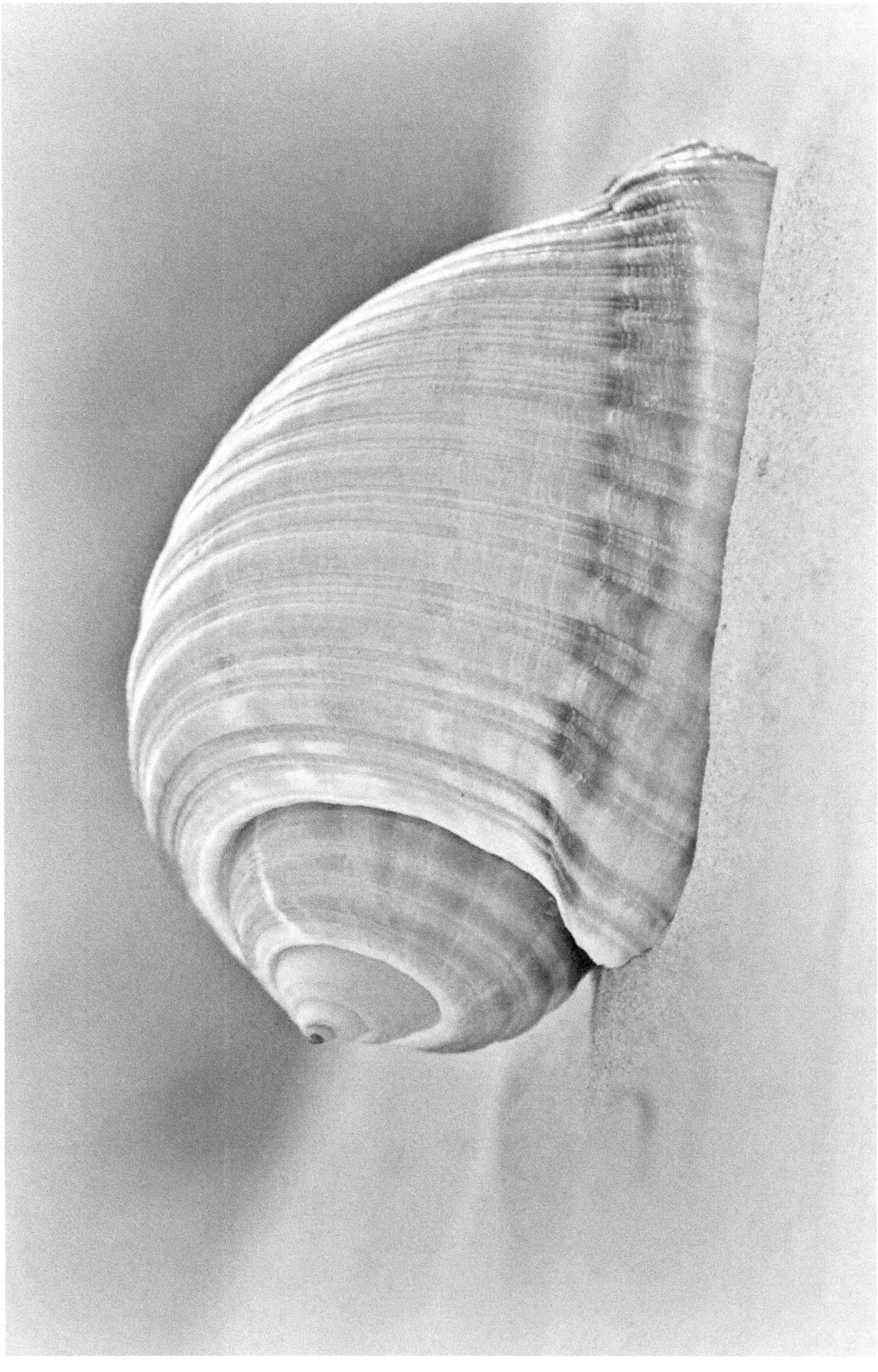

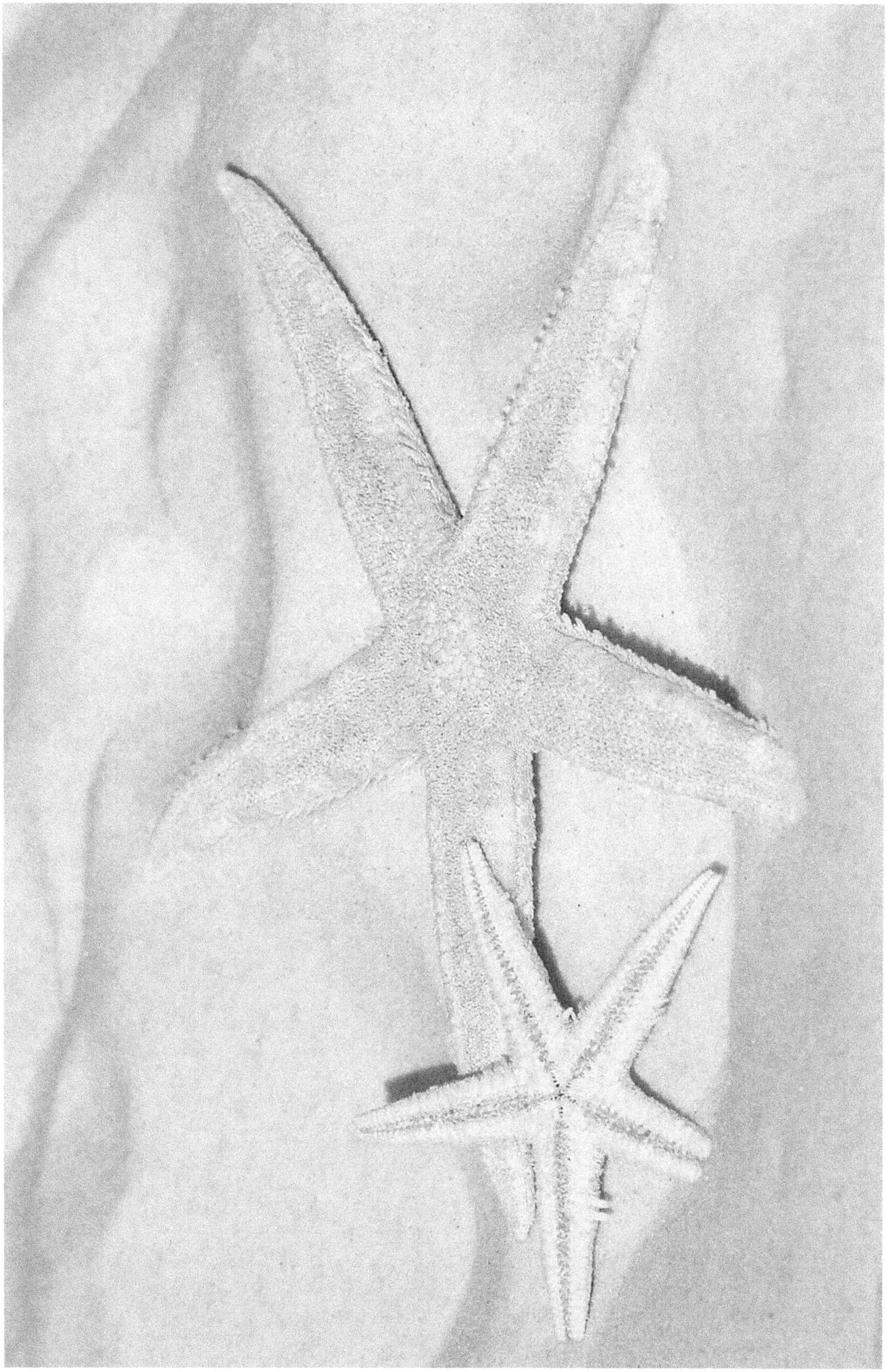

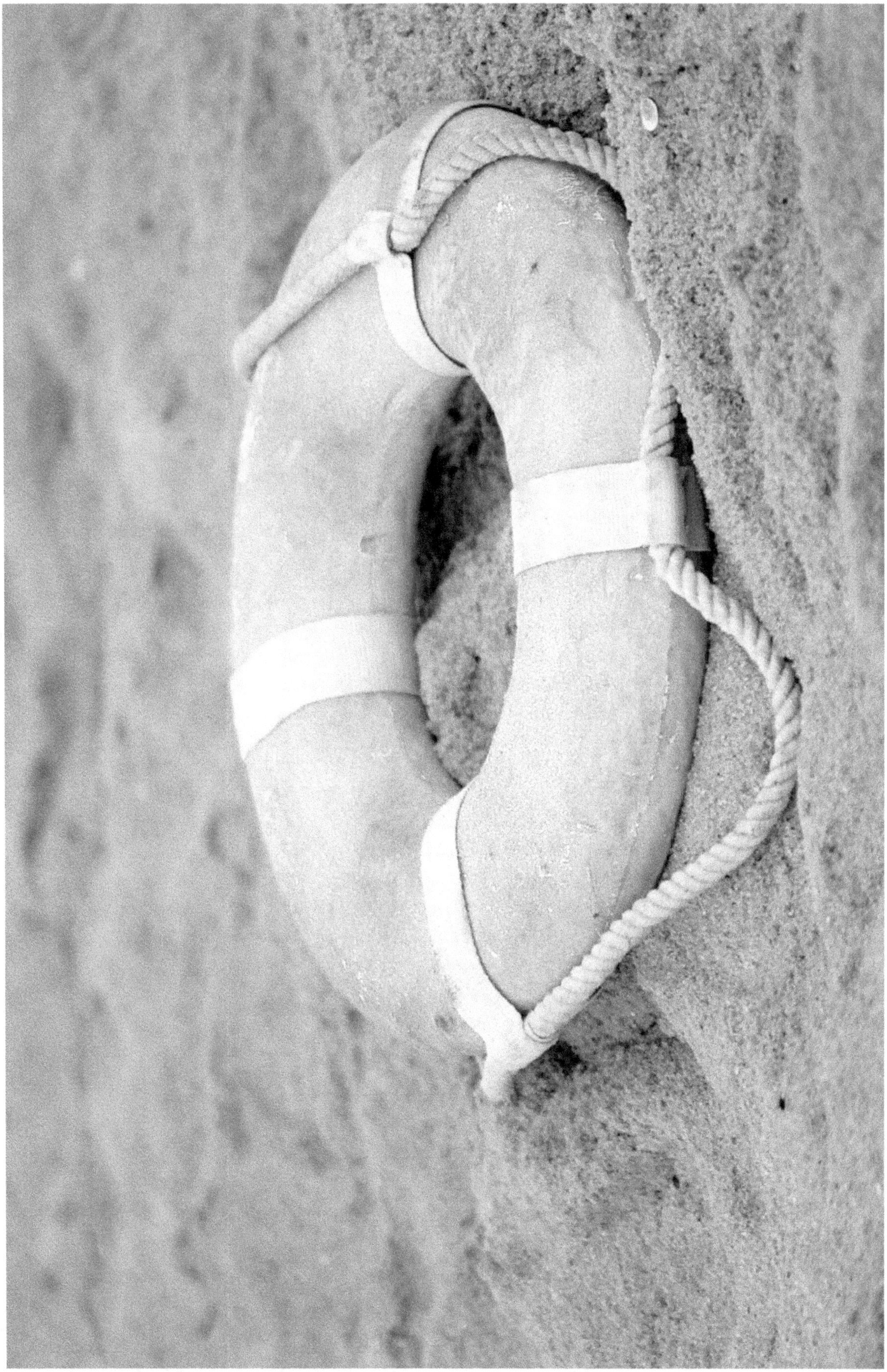

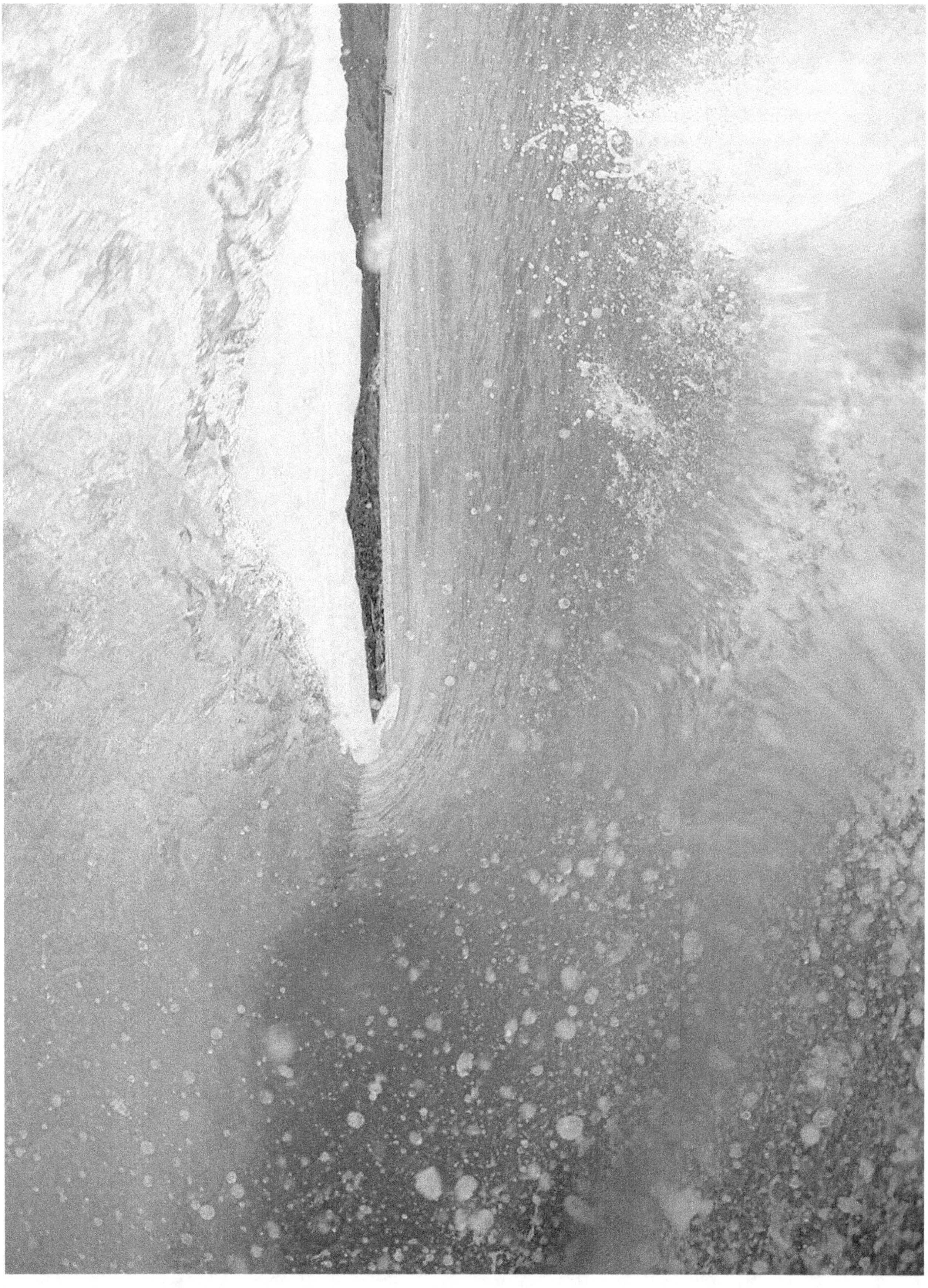

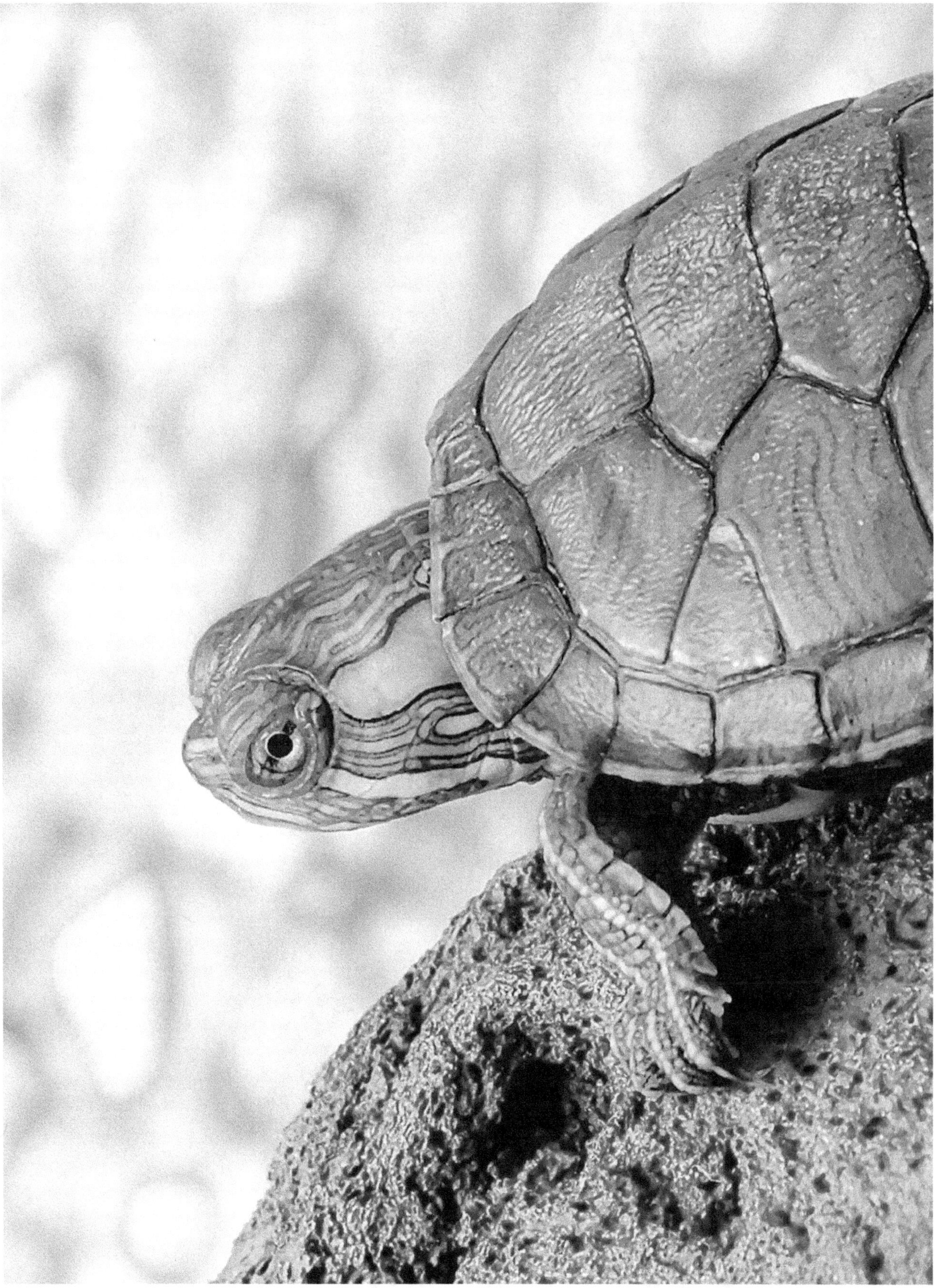

www.ingramcontent.com/pod-product-compliance
Lightning Source LLC
Chambersburg PA
CBHW081120280526
45787CB00007B/2920
* 9 7 8 1 5 3 5 2 2 8 2 9 9 *